A BASKET OF
APPLES

JAMES GRIEVE

WORCESTER PEARMAIN

GOLDEN NOBLE

BLENHEIM ORANGE

APPLES

DEVONSHIRE QUARRENDEN

A BASKET OF
APPLES

Recipes and paintings from
a country orchard

VAL ARCHER

HARMONY BOOKS
NEW YORK

Published by Harmony Books, a division of Crown
Publishers, Inc., 201 East 50th Street, New York, New
York 10022.
Member of the Crown Publishing Group.
Random House, Inc., New York, Toronto, London,
Sydney, Auckland

Originally published in Great Britain in 1993 by
Pavilion Books Limited.

HARMONY and colophon are trademarks of
Crown Publishers, Inc.

Manufactured in Italy

Library of Congress Cataloging-in-Publication Data is
available from the publisher.

ISBN 0–517–59622–9

1 3 5 7 9 10 8 6 4 2

First American Edition

CONTENTS

INTRODUCTION

There is an apple tree outside our kitchen window in London. It was one of the reasons why we bought our house. All my life I've lived close to apple trees; my mum says when she was first married, there was an apple tree by the back door. It was old, gnarled, bent and nameless, but produced crisp golden apples of unimaginable sweetness. She spent the autumn before I was born sitting and peeling away the skin in unbroken strands, which fell around her ankles in yellow ringlets. She made crusty pies, dumplings, jelly and sweet, spicy chutney. The perfect apples were carefully wrapped in sheets from the *Chronicle* and *Echo* and stored in the loft, but they tasted best when eaten straight from the tree; my mother would sometimes creep down in the middle of the night to stand munching in the silent garden.

The first things that my father planted when they moved house when I was two were five apple trees: a Bramley for cooking; a Worcester Pearmain for early reds; a biannual Laxton Superb; a Cox's Orange Pippin, which disliked its designated position against the barn wall, only occasionally and

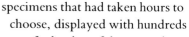

grudgingly producing a couple of misshapen fruits; and, in the centre of the garden, a generous and abundant Charles Ross. It was this tree that gave my Dad his prizewinning exhibits at the local show, three perfect specimens that had taken hours to choose, displayed with hundreds of other hopefuls on trestle tables covered with white paper in a marquee smelling of crushed grass and dahlias. The excitement, which began with placing the fruit, mounted as the tent was re-opened after the judging; we made our way down avenues of onions, their tops bound with raffia and standing on piles of silver sand, bunches of carrots, green leaves fanned out like horses' tails, jars of honey, bottles of home-made wine, and the curled heads of huge white chrysanthemums (just released from their protective brown paper bags) to the apple section. And in 'Category: dessert' there it would be, the red card, first prize again for Mr D. Archer.

Apples grow whenever sunny days turn the flesh sweet, and cold nights give blushing colour and a good bite. Before the Romans came we had only small, hard, wild crab apples, but they loved apples so much, they thought that the perfect meal began with eggs and ended with apples (*ab ovo usque ad onaia*) and took domestic varieties to be planted in the farthest corners of the Roman Empire to satisfy their appetite.

The Pilgrim Fathers took apple pips with them to the New World to establish the domestic apple there. In the eighteenth century John Chapman from Massachusetts became known as Johnny Appleseed for his habit of filling his pockets with apple seeds discarded by the cider mills and planting orchards wherever he went.

In England in the early 1800s Thomas Knight of Herefordshire brought about a revolution in apple- breeding. He began a series of experiments in pollination, becoming the first man to raise apples whose parentage was known. He produced a new range of successful apple varieties and, under his encouragement, fruit- breeding became a passion among both amateur and professional gardeners. The world-famous Cox's Orange Pippin resulted from one such controlled pollination by an amateur, the eponymous Mr Cox.

Thomas Laxton, a disciple of Thomas Knight, was the most successful of all nurserymen. He began with experiments on hybridizing pears for Charles Darwin and later turned his attention to apples. His work was carried on by his sons, who ten years later had a stock of 10,000 different varieties of apple, plum and pear, the main source of Britain's present selection of 4,000 apple varieties.

I was especially nervous about painting apples, for the greatest artists have celebrated their simple pleasures. The first known paintings of apples are preserved on the walls of a Roman Villa in Pompeii, and from then on, almost every century has had its apple painters. I remember from my first visit to the National Gallery the joy I felt on finding, in so grand a place, with such a selection of elevated subject matter, Courbet's modest plate of apples. The pictures I respond to most enthusiastically are the ones painted for the pure enjoyment of apples, almost as if the artists are eating them with their eyes.

If you read this book without an apple in your hand, I hope it makes you want to go and find one; and remember, when you take the first bite, the Romans and Johnny Appleseed, Mr Cox and Thomas Laxton, and all the quiet men and women who found a wonderful apple tree in their garden and shared its seeds.

HORTICULTURAL NOTES

You don't need an orchard to grow apple trees; trees of all varieties can be grown in small as well as large spaces, from tubs to fields. If you buy a young tree from a nursery, sample the fruit first, so you know you will enjoy the apples you grow.

Apple varieties are propagated by grafting the chosen variety on to a rootstock. There is a wide range of rootstocks, classified according to vigour as the rootstock influences the size of the mature tree. A variety grafted on to vigorous stock grows into a large tree, whereas the same variety grafted on to a dwarfing stock remains small. At the nursery where you make your purchase there will be a selection of trees from which you can choose already grafted on to rootstock. Another factor to consider is the condition of your soil; if it is poor, dwarfing stock will need regular fertilizing and watering to yield a reasonable crop of apples, so a vigorous stock would be a better choice, as the poor soil conditions will naturally limit the size to which the tree can grow.

If you have a small garden, avoid the more vigorous growing varieties. A standard tree grown to its full height of 6–7.5m/20–25ft produces 90–180kg/200–400lbs of fruit each season. A dwarf tree will grow to a height of

1.8m/6ft and yield about 18kg/40lbs of fruit, plenty for a small family. An espalier is decoratively trained against a wall or fence and could produce 9–13kg/20–30lbs once mature. A step-over is an espalier trained along a 30cm/12 inch high support, which can be used as an edging for borders and beds. One bush will give 2.3–2.7kg/5–6lbs of apples, but usually you would plant more than one to make a long low hedge. A Ballerina tree is a compact column that was introduced in 1989. It grows with no side branches to 2.4m/8ft high, producing 4.5–9kg/ 10–20lbs of fruit when fully grown.

If apple trees are not common in your area, a single tree will not bear fruit unless it has a partner of a different variety growing near by which flowers at the same time and will pollinate it. You could grow instead a family tree which has two to four different varieties of apple grafted on to one rootstock; not only do you have an extended crop, but also cross-pollination is ensured. You can choose family trees which combine both dessert and culinary varieties, but be warned, they need careful pruning to prevent the most vigorous grower from dominating the rest.

Some apple varieties can be grown on extremely dwarfing rootstocks to produce a tree or bush so small that it can be pot-grown on a patio or balcony, and these are usefully portable if you move house or if a hard frost threatens at blossom-time.

Apple trees grow best in open, sunny, sheltered positions in all but the most chalky soil conditions. Ideally they like well-drained, slightly acid soils which don't dry out too quickly, though they are not keen on having their roots waterlogged.

There are comprehensive books available on apple-growing, which give detailed instructions on planting, fertilizing, pruning and spraying. They also give advice about the varieties and types that would suit your garden, such as late-flowering trees for frost-prone gardens, or scab-resistant cultivars for organic growers living in marshy areas. A similar space could support either one vigorously growing standard tree or two to three different varieties of dwarf tree, giving you apples from August to October. As a rule, early fruiting varieties produce apples that are best eaten straight from the tree. Late harvesters produce good storing apples, some types keeping well into April.

HARVESTING AND STORING

At harvest–time, test whether each apple is ready to pick by placing it in the palm of your hand and simultaneously lifting and twisting. If it is ripe, it will come away easily with the stalk attached. Fruit for storing should not be over-ripe, contain insect blemishes, or be bruised, so handle it carefully. Early varieties are best eaten straight off the tree. Mid–season apples will keep for a few weeks but late varieties will last for months. Some, like D'Arcy Spice, improve with keeping.

Each apple should be wrapped in paper and placed folded-side down in a single layer on fibre trays, or placed in clear plastic bags, 2.25kg/5lb to each bag, with the bags perforated and the tops folded but not sealed. Don't store different varieties in the same bag or box. Store the apples in a frost-free, well-ventilated room or outhouse where the temperature is stable and cool. Check regularly for signs of mould. Rotten fruit should be removed immediately or others will be affected.

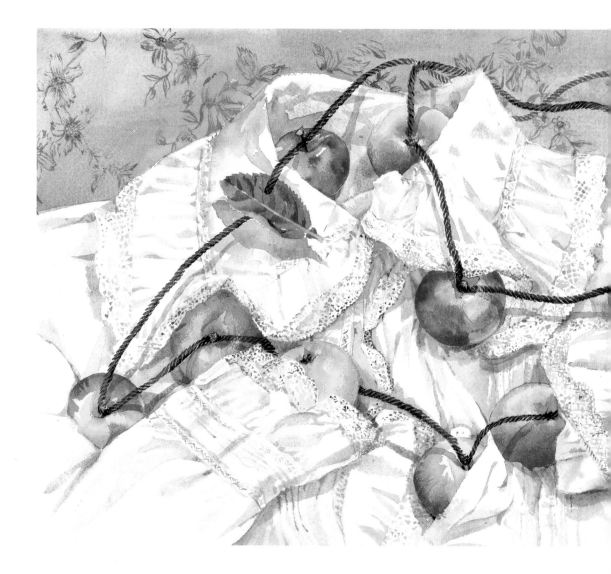

APPLE CURD

The Lady apple or Pomme d'Api is bright red on one side and
creamy white on the other, the perfect colour combination it was thought for a lady's
cheeks. Was it for this reason that it was given its charming name,
or because its strongly scented skin made it an ideal companion for the quince to
perfume stored linen and night-dresses? The old way of drying
apples was to peel, core and thread them whole, then hang them up like necklaces.

*350g/12oz cooking apples
(weighed after peeling and coring)
1 lemon
45g/1½oz/3 tbsp unsalted butter
120g/4oz/generous ½ cup caster
(superfine) sugar
2 egg yolks*

Slice the apples and cook gently until tender with the juice and zest of lemon. Rub through a sieve. Put this purée in the top of a double boiler and add the butter, sugar and beaten yolks. Stir over gently boiling water until the yolks thicken the mixture. Remove from the heat at once and pour into small pots. Cover immediately and store in the refrigerator when cold. This curd will not keep for long, so it is best made in small quantities. Serve it for breakfast, spread on toasted walnut bread, English muffins or croissants.

Makes 500g/1lb 2oz

MUESLI

250g/8oz/1 cup ready-to-eat prunes
250g/8oz/1 cup ready-to-eat dried apricots
175g/6oz/1½ cups sultanas (golden raisins)
250g/8oz/1½ cups hazelnuts
120g/4oz/¾ cup sunflower seeds
700g/1½lb/4½ cups mixed jumbo oats,
regular oats, wheat, barley and rye flakes

Preheat oven to 200°C/400°F/Gas 6.

Roast the hazelnuts and chop them coarsely. Chop the dried fruit into smallish chunks. Spread the oats, grains and sunflower seeds on a large baking tray and carefully roast in the oven, turning frequently until they are golden brown.

Leave until cool, then mix all the ingredients together in a large bowl. Transfer to an air-tight storage jar.

Serve with natural yogurt, milk or fruit juice, adding a freshly chopped apple just before serving. (The Empire apple's red-skinned crescents look especially pretty.)

APPLE MUFFINS

The smell of freshly baked muffins for breakfast is enticing, and they
are wonderful served hot with apple curd. Alternative additions to the basic apple
mixture could include cranberry and orange, blackberries,
blueberries, or chopped dried apricots with walnuts.

300ml/10fl oz/1¼ cups skimmed milk
120g/4oz/1 cup oat bran
2 eggs
75g/2½oz/5 tbsp butter, melted
45g/1½oz/3 tbsp light brown sugar
½ tsp vanilla extract
· 60g/2oz/½ cup wholemeal flour

120g/4oz/1 cup plain (all-purpose) flour
½ tsp salt
2 tsp baking powder
1 eating apple, peeled, cored and chopped
2 tbsp raisins soaked in rum or orange juice
30g/1oz/¼ cup toasted chopped
pecan nuts

Preheat the oven to 190°C/375°F/Gas 5.
Grease 12 muffin tins with extra butter.

Place the milk and oat bran in a bowl and set
aside. Beat together the eggs, melted butter,
sugar and vanilla extract. In another bowl
mix the flours, salt and baking powder. Add
the apple to the flour mixture, stirring to coat
it as you go. Mix the soaked oat bran with the
egg mixture then roughly stir in the apple and
dry ingredients. Divide into two, stirring the
raisins into one half, the pecans into the other.
Put a heaped dessertspoonful into each muffin
tin and bake for 25–30 minutes until risen and
golden brown.

Makes 6 of each flavour

FRIED APPLE AND FRENCH TOAST

Grilled tomatoes and spiced sausages are another delicious breakfast
combination to serve with the apple and French toast.

2 large dessert apples
45g/1½oz/3 tbsp butter
8 slices of bread
1 egg
a pinch of dried sage
salt and freshly ground black pepper
8 rashers (strips) of bacon
black pudding

Peel and core the apples and slice into
rings. Fry in half the butter on both sides
until golden brown.

To make the French toast, cut rounds of
bread the same size as the apple rings, using
a pastry cutter.

Beat the egg together with the sage, salt
and pepper. Soak the bread rounds in this
then fry in the remaining butter on both sides
until brown. Put the fried apple on top of the
French toast and keep warm.

Meanwhile fry the bacon until crisp. Cut
the black pudding into slices and fry in the
rendered bacon fat on both sides.

To serve, put two apple toasts,
two rashers of bacon and
pieces of black pudding
on to each hot plate.

Serves 4

APPLE AND FENNEL SOUP

This clean-tasting soup is best made with dessert apples as cooking
apples are too sour. It can be served cold in summer with the addition of Greek
yogurt and hot in winter with soured cream.

30g/1oz/2 tbsp unsalted butter
1 medium onion, peeled and chopped
2 medium fennel bulbs, chopped
4 apples, peeled, cored and chopped
1 litre/32fl oz/1 quart vegetable or
chicken stock
3 tbsp Greek yogurt or soured cream
flaked almonds, for garnish

Melt the butter in a non-stick saucepan and fry the onion until it is transparent, not coloured. Add the chopped fennel and apple, and fry with the onion for 2 minutes. Add one third of the stock and cook gently until cooked, about 20 minutes.

Allow to cool then put in a blender with the remaining stock and process until smooth. You can then pour it through a sieve if you want an especially smooth soup.

To serve cold, stir in the yogurt and chill. Pour into bowls and garnish with flaked almonds. To serve hot, reheat to just below boiling point, pour into warmed soup bowls, swirl a little soured cream into each bowl and sprinkle with flaked almonds.

Serves 6

APPLE AND BEETROOT BORTSCH

2 tbsp melted butter
1 medium onion, peeled and chopped
1 large carrot, peeled and
coarsely grated
2 sticks of celery, thinly sliced
450g/1lb raw beetroot, peeled and
coarsely grated
350g/12oz red cabbage,
coarsely grated
1 bouquet garni
2 tbsp cider vinegar

400g/14oz/about 3 cups peeled and
chopped tomatoes, or 1×400g/
1×14oz can tomatoes
1.2 litres/2 pints/4½ cups
vegetable stock
2 dessert apples, peeled, cored
and grated
1 tsp dried dill
½ raw beetroot, peeled (optional)
salt and freshly ground black pepper
soured cream

In a large saucepan fry the onion in the butter until transparent. Add the carrot and celery, and fry for 1 minute. Add the beetroot and cabbage to the saucepan with the bouquet garni. Pour in the chopped tomatoes, cider vinegar and stock, cover, bring to the boil and simmer for 30 minutes. Add the apple and dried dill, and cook for a further 10 minutes or until cabbage and beetroot are cooked but not mushy.

Turn off the heat, pour half of the soup into the liquidizer and process until smooth. Pour back into the saucepan and combine with the grated ingredients so the soup is thick but still has a texture. If the soup has lost its brilliant magenta colour, at this stage you can stir in some finely grated raw beetroot to make the colour return. Adjust the seasoning and reheat without boiling. Serve in bowls with a swirl of soured cream in each.

Serves 6

APPLE SANDWICHES

The first recipe is one which Arabella Boxer has adapted from *Lady Sysonby's Cookbook* and, as she says, it is refreshing on a hot summer's day. In the second recipe, apple replaces the butter or mayonnaise usually added to a smoked fish pâté.

8 thin slices brown bread
30g/1oz/2 tbsp unsalted butter, softened
3-4 tbsp mayonnaise
2 Granny Smith apples, cored and cut in quarters

Spread four slices of bread with butter and the other four with mayonnaise. Slice the unpeeled apple quarters thinly and lay them on the buttered bread. Cover with the mayonnaised bread. Remove the crusts and cut each sandwich in quarters.

Toss the apple in the lemon juice. Add the
fish fillets to the apple, and mash together
with the horseradish. Add lots of freshly
ground pepper and salt to taste. Spread the
bread thinly with butter and make
sandwiches as usual. Remove crusts and cut
each sandwich in quarters.

*1 Granny Smith, cored, peeled and
grated coarsely
juice of ½ lemon
175g/6oz smoked trout or mackerel
fillets, skinned
2 tsp grated horseradish
salt and freshly ground black pepper
8 thin slices granary bread
30g/1oz/2 tbsp unsalted butter, softened*

Each makes 16 small sandwiches

WILTED SPINACH SALAD WITH APPLE AND FETA CHEESE

This is a good starter to serve before a simple main course such as
grilled fish or meat.

1 clove garlic, peeled and crushed
4 spring onions (scallions), trimmed
and sliced diagonally
1 tbsp fresh mint chopped with
1 tsp sugar
2 tbsp lemon juice
freshly ground black pepper
1 large dessert apple (Cox), cored,
quartered and sliced thinly
175g/6oz Feta cheese
250g/8oz young spinach leaves with
stalks removed
2½ tbsp light olive oil
3 tbsp pine kernels

Mix the first six ingredients in a large salad
bowl, and crumble the Feta on top.

Wash the spinach thoroughly, tear the larger
leaves into smaller pieces, then drain and dry
well. Put on top of the cheese in the bowl
without tossing.

Heat the olive oil in a saucepan, add the pine
kernels and continue to heat until the kernels
turn golden brown. Pour the hot oil and the
kernels over the spinach and toss the whole
salad thoroughly.

The hot oil should slightly cook the spinach
leaves and all the ingredients should be evenly
distributed through the salad. Adjust the
seasoning and serve immediately with hot
French bread.

Serves 6 as a starter, 4 as a supper dish

WALDORF SALAD

Waldorf salad can look a bit dull. Although not authentic, it seems more
colourful served on leaves of radicchio. Use red-skinned apples, and for a change
throw in a handful or two of seedless grapes.

250g/8oz celery, trimmed weight
250g/8oz red-skinned crisp apples
120-175g/4-6oz/1-1¼ cups shelled
walnuts, broken in 2-3 pieces
125g/4oz seedless grapes
3 tbsp mayonnaise
3 tbsp low-fat natural yogurt
salt
a few celery leaves
4-8 whole walnut pieces
radicchio leaves

Wash the celery and slice it fairly thinly.
Quarter and core the apples and cut into dice.
Put into a bowl with the broken walnuts and
seedless grapes.

Mix the mayonnaise with the yogurt to thin
it, then season to taste and pour over the
apples and celery. Toss so that everything is
coated with thin mayonnaise, then turn into a
decorative bowl and garnish with celery
leaves and whole walnut pieces. Serve from
the bowl, heaped on to radicchio leaves.

Serves 4

APPLE, MUSHROOM, FENNEL AND PARMESAN SALAD

1 clove garlic, peeled
¼ tsp coarse sea salt
½ tsp fennel seeds
finely grated rind of ½ lemon
2½ tbsp lemon juice
4-5 tbsp extra virgin olive oil
175g/6oz mushrooms, wiped clean
and thinly sliced

freshly ground black pepper
1 large red-skinned apple, cored,
quartered and thinly sliced
1 fennel bulb
90g/3oz Parmesan Reggiano cheese,
shaved from block
fennel leaves, to garnish

Pound the garlic and salt in a mortar, then add the fennel seeds and crush. Stir in the lemon rind, lemon juice and olive oil. Dress the mushrooms with two thirds of this dressing, and season with freshly ground black pepper. Gently toss the apple slices with the mushrooms in the dressing, cover and leave for at least 30 minutes to marinate.

Trim the fennel bulb and quarter it. Slice thinly, leaving the pieces joined together. Mix with the remaining dressing and add to the mushrooms and apples.

To serve, spoon the salad on to individual plates and shave Parmesan cheese on top. Finish with a few fennel fronds and a turn of black pepper.

Serves 4 as a starter

APPLE, WATERCRESS AND MARIGOLD SALAD

1 tbsp orange juice
3 tbsp walnut oil
salt and freshly ground black pepper
1 bunch of watercress
2 heads of chicory (endive)
2 dessert apples, cored, quartered and
thinly sliced
1 marigold
2 tbsp roasted walnut pieces

Make a dressing with the orange juice, walnut oil, salt and pepper.

Remove the tough stalks from the watercress, then wash and dry thoroughly. Cut the base from the chicory and separate the leaves (it usually does not need washing). Make a bed of watercress on a round plate and arrange the chicory leaves in a star shape on top.

Toss the apple slices in the dressing, drain and place on top of the chicory. Pull the petals from the marigold and scatter over the salad with the walnut pieces. Drizzle more dressing over the salad and serve as soon as possible.

Serves 4 as a side salad

APPLE, BEETROOT AND
HERRING SALAD

250g/8oz pickled herring
300g/10oz waxy potatoes peeled,
cooked and diced
2 large dessert apples, peeled and cored
and diced

outside of an oval plate, put the beetroot into the middle and place the herring strips on top. Scatter with parsley and chill. Combine the soured cream, vinegar, mustard and seasoning and serve separately.

1 small onion, thinly sliced in rings
450g/1lb boiled beetroot, peeled and diced
3 tbsp dressing made with oil and
lemon juice
chopped parsley
150ml/5fl oz/⅔ cup soured cream
1 dsp wine vinegar
1 tsp Dijon mustard
salt and freshly ground black pepper

Cut the herring into 2.5cm/1 inch thick strips. Combine the potato, apple and onion in a bowl with 2 tbsp of the dressing. In a separate bowl mix the beetroot with the remaining dressing. Leave to stand.

  Half an hour before serving, arrange the apple, onion and potato around the

Serves 4

GRILLED TUNA KEBABS

If fresh tuna is unavailable use any firm fish as a substitute. Salmon, monkfish, swordfish, shark or halibut are all suitable, as they are meaty enough not to fall apart.

1kg/2lb fresh tuna
1 small onion, peeled and grated
juice of ½ lemon
1 clove garlic, peeled and crushed
2 tbsp ground cumin
4 tbsp olive oil
salt and freshly ground black pepper

Mix the grated onion, lemon juice, garlic, cumin, oil, salt and pepper in a large shallow bowl. Cut the fish into 4 cm/1½ inch cubes, put the fish into the bowl. Cover and marinate for at least 1 hour in the refrigerator turning the fish at intervals.

Preheat the grill or barbecue. Thread the fish on to four kebab skewers and cook on an oiled rack, turning two or three times and brushing them with the marinade at the same time, until brown and cooked. Take care not to overcook. Serve immediately with apple salsa on the side.

Apple Salsa

Apple salsa is a kind of uncooked chutney. Tasting fresh and zingy it's perfect on grilled or barbecued fish. It keeps in the refrigerator for up to a week, though it stays sparkling green for only a couple of hours. It's great swirled into soups or pasta, or stirred into cottage cheese to fill a baked potato.

45g/1½oz/¾ cup fresh coriander
leaves and some stems
30g/1oz/½ cup fresh mint leaves
175g/6oz Granny Smith apple,
peeled, cored and chopped
grated rind and juice of 2 limes
2 garlic cloves, peeled
1 green chilli, deseeded and chopped
1 tsp caster (superfine) sugar
3 tbsp light olive oil

Wash and dry the mint and coriander. Put into food processor with apple, lime juice and rind, garlic, chilli and sugar, and process until well chopped, gradually adding the olive oil. Season with salt. Cover and refrigerate.

Makes 250ml/8fl oz/1 cup

STIR-FRIED PRAWNS, SNOW PEAS AND APPLE

Fresh prawns are quick to cook and look marvellous combined with bright green mangetout or snow peas and golden apples (try to use a yellow-fleshed apple that stays firm while cooking).

450g/1lb fresh uncooked prawns
2 tbsp vegetable oil
1 tbsp coarsely grated fresh root ginger
1 tbsp chopped garlic
150g/5oz snow peas, topped and tailed
2 dessert apples, quartered, cored and
sliced and tossed in juice of ½ lemon

5 spring onions (scallions), cut in shreds
lengthwise then in 2.5cm/1inch pieces
2 tsp sesame oil

FOR THE MARINADE
1 tsp salt
½ tsp chilli oil (if liked)
1 tsp sesame oil

Mix together the marinade ingredients in a shallow bowl.

Peel the prawns, leaving the little tail section intact. Using a sharp knife, partially split the prawns lengthways along their upper edge and remove the dark digestive cord. Dry the prawns, toss in the marinade and leave for half an hour.

Heat the vegetable oil in a preheated wok or large frying pan (skillet), add ginger, garlic and prawns and stir-fry for 30 seconds. Add snow peas and stir-fry for 1 minute. Add apples and stir-fry for 1 minute. Add spring onions, sesame oil and 2 tbsp of water. Stir-fry for 2 minutes and serve with rice.

Serves 2 as a main course, 4 as a starter

APPLE RISOTTO

2 tbsp olive oil
1 small onion, peeled and chopped
700ml/2 pints/scant 3 cups vegetable
or chicken stock
300g/10oz Arborio rice
350g/12oz dessert apple, peeled and diced
salt and freshly ground black pepper
60g/2oz/²⁄₃ cup freshly grated
Parmesan cheese

Heat the olive oil in a saucepan and sauté onion until it is lightly coloured. Bring the stock to simmering point in another saucepan. Add the rice to the onion and sauté for one minute so each grain is coated with oil. Add the apple, stir and cook for a further minute, pour in a ladleful of stock and stir while cooking. When that has been absorbed, add another 150ml/¼ pint/²⁄₃ cup of simmering stock and continue to cook, stirring constantly, repeating until the rice is tender but firm (regulate heat so that the cooking process takes about 30 minutes). The rice should be *al dente*, firm to bite and creamily bound together, neither dry nor runny.

Turn off the heat, add salt and black pepper to taste. Stir in grated cheese and, if liked, an ounce of unsalted butter. Serve at once with extra cheese on the table.

Serves 4

Allington Pippin *Mid to late dessert apple. Hardy trees which fruit in cold conditions, so suitable for northern gardens. Rich aromatic flavour, creamy white juicy flesh.*

Blenheim Orange *The classic Christmas apple, crisp and acid with pale yellow aromatic flesh. Sweet fruit-and-nut flavour develops with keeping.*

Beauty of Bath *An old-fashioned early dessert apple. Flesh sweet, aromatic and juicy. It is rather coarse-textured and soft and does not keep well.*

Bramley's Seedling *Very large and green, can have faint red stripes. Creamy, juicy acid flesh, cooks to a smooth purée, best for apple sauce.*

Charles Ross *Large dessert/ cooking apple best early in the season when sharply flavoured and juicy. Later in season skin turns deep yellow with musky odour.*

Chiver's Delight *Late dessert apple, keeps well and retains shape when cooked. Aromatic and sweet, not too acid – truly a delight.*

Cox's Orange Pippin *Excellent for cooking, imparts strong flavour and retains shape. Skin contains much aromatic flavour so should be eaten.*

Discovery *Very early British dessert apple, skin bright green and crimson. White flesh, pinkish near the red skin. Light and crisp, it does not keep, best eaten chilled when flesh has slight raspberry taste.*

Egremont Russet *Rough golden brown russetted skin, white hard flesh, nutty autumnal flavour, wonderful with cheese, also good cooked in tarts and pies.*

Empire *American dessert apple with deep red skin and round shape. Crisp green tinged flesh, juicy with light, clean taste. McIntosh hybrid.*

Fiesta *A new dessert apple; Cox crossed with Ida Red. Fruit larger than Cox. All the aroma and nuttiness of Cox but easier to grow. Crisp and juicy, it cooks well.*

Gala *Raised in New Zealand, tough yellowish skin, becomes more flushed red with sunshine. Sweet, crisp yellow flesh, cooks well.*

Golden Delicious *An American seedling discovered in 1900. Good all-round apple.*

Gravenstein *Large American apple. Crisp, juicy, rather acid when eaten but good for cooking.*

Granny Smith *Hard, tart and refreshing. Good for sorbets. Cooks well, retaining sharp flavour.*

Greening *American, long-season apple, crisp, sharp and acid it cooks well, but also good to eat.*

Jonathan *American apple, tough orange skin heavily streaked with bright red. Crisp but softens quickly, so eat fresh. Dessert apple, but good cooked in tarts.*

Jonagold *Large apple, yellow toughish skin overlaid with green and red. Creamy white flesh, full-flavoured, sweet and juicy. Keeps and cooks well.*

James Grieve *Early dessert apple. Sweet with good acid balance, can be used as a cooker in July. Keeps until Christmas, becomes soft but flavour still good.*

Ida Red *Late ripening apple with good keeping qualities. White flesh tastes sweet and winey. A fine crisp, juicy dessert apple but thin flavour.*

Lady Apple *Also called pomme d'Api. Small, pretty, with red and creamy yellow skin, sweet white flesh.*

Laxton Superb *Sweet dessert apple. Pale greenish yellow half-covered with dull crimson, toughish skin. White-green tinged flesh, crisp but slightly watery.*

Newton Pippin *Found on Long Island in 1700. Yellowish green, keeps well, good acidity, though can be mealy. Cooking or dessert apple.*

Lord Derby *Mid to late cooking apple, which does not disintegrate. Best eaten when green. Greenish-white coarse-textured flesh.*

McIntosh *Red with green-tinged skin. Juicy, sweet, white, crisp flesh, slightly tart. Good for apple sauce and pies as well as dessert.*

Northern Spy *Very versatile American apple, rich flavour good for baked apples, pies and sauces.*

Orleans Rienette *Large golden russet, rough and flecked orange. Flesh very juicy, fine textured, firm and sweet-tasting.*

Rome Beauty *American cooking apple with bright red skin. Juicy and stays crisp for a long time. Flavour weak. Keeps its shape well when baked.*

Spartan *Crisp white raspberry-flavoured flesh. Very sweet, must be eaten fresh. Cooks well.*

Sturmer Pippin *Excellent dessert and cooking apple. Firm, fine-textured, tart, juicy flesh.*

Winesap *American, often used as cider apple. Crisp rich-flavoured flesh. Good to eat and cook.*

Worcester Pearmain *White juicy flesh with hints of straw-berry.*

PHEASANT WITH CALVADOS AND APPLES

This is quite a rich dish, a traditional recipe from Normandy, the home of Calvados and cider. All you need to serve with it is a few plainly cooked potatoes and a green salad.

1 young oven-ready roasting pheasant
120g/4oz/½ cup butter
1kg/2lb firm, well-flavoured dessert
apples, peeled, cored and sliced
ground cinnamon
4 tbsp Calvados
250ml/8fl oz/1 cup double
(heavy) cream
salt and freshly ground black pepper

Cook the pheasant gently in half of the butter in a heavy iron pan on top of the stove for about 40–45 minutes, covered. Turn it occasionally to brown all sides. The bird is cooked if the juices run clear when you test between breast and leg with a skewer.

Meanwhile, fry the apples until golden in the remaining butter. Sprinkle them with a little cinnamon and keep warm.

Remove the pheasant from the heat and pour the juices into a small pan. Carve the bird, place it on a warmed serving dish and keep warm while you finish the sauce.

Place the pan with the cooking juices over a low heat and allow them to bubble gently while you warm the Calvados in a small pan. Set light to the spirit and pour it into the juices, shaking the pan until the flames die down. Add the cream, raise the heat slightly and stir well until the sauce thickens. Do not boil. Season to taste.

Arrange the apples around the pheasant and spoon over the sauce or pass it separately, if you prefer.

Serves 2–3

DUCK BREASTS
WITH
LENTILS AND APPLE

This recipe is a good way of serving the beautiful
French Puy lentils.

4 duck breasts
225g/8oz Puy lentils
(or any small, brown lentils)
1 small onion, peeled and stuck with 3 cloves
1 bay leaf

a sprig of thyme
30g/1oz/2 tbsp butter
1 dessert apple, peeled, cored and diced
1 clove garlic, peeled and crushed
2 tbsp sunflower oil

Put the lentils, onion, bay leaf and
thyme in a saucepan, and add enough
water to cover the lentils plus 2.5
cm/1 inch. Bring to the boil, then
simmer, covered, for 25 minutes or
until cooked. They should remain
whole.

Heat the butter in a frying pan, add
the apple and crushed garlic, and stir
until lightly cooked.

Drain the lentils. Remove the onion
and herbs. Add the lentils to the apple
in the frying pan and reheat gently.

Rub the duck breasts on both sides
with the oil, then place them skin side
up under a preheated grill. Cook for 7
minutes on the first side then turn and
cook for another 4 minutes on the
second side. Remove from heat and
leave to cool a little. Divide the lentil
mixture between four warm plates,
slice the duck breasts diagonally and
place on top of the lentils. Serve with a
green salad.

STEAMED SPICED CHICKEN BREASTS

Steaming keeps the lean chicken breast moist, and the marinade
imparts an exotic flavour in this healthy recipe, which can be served with glazed
carrots and apples (see p. 55).

4 chicken breasts, boned and skinned
2 spring onions (scallions), sliced

FOR THE MARINADE
4 tsp coriander seeds
1 tsp black peppercorns
½ tsp sea salt
2 large cloves garlic, peeled
375ml/12fl oz/1½ cups cider
1 tbsp sesame oil

For the marinade, heat the coriander seeds
and peppercorns in a non-stick pan until they
begin to brown and the seeds pop. Grind the
salt and garlic to a purée with a pestle and
mortar, then add the toasted coriander and
pepper and grind to a coarse powder. Pour
the cider into the pan and boil until it is
reduced by half (to intensify the flavour).
Add this to the spices along with the
sesame oil.

Make four diagonal cuts across each
chicken breast, put into a shallow dish,
and pour over the marinade. Cover and
refrigerate for at least 2 hours, basting
with the marinade from time to time.

Half-fill the bottom of a steamer with
water and bring to the boil over a high heat.

Place the top half of the steamer over the
water, making sure no water comes through
the holes. (You can use a bamboo steaming
basket, placed over water in a wok or frying
pan.) Put a heatproof plate in the steamer.
Take the chicken breasts out of the marinade,
place on the plate, and sprinkle with sliced
spring onions. Cover and steam for 10–15
minutes, or until the juices run clear. Serve at
once with a little of the cooking juices poured
over them and a portion of glazed carrots and
apples to the side.

Serves 4

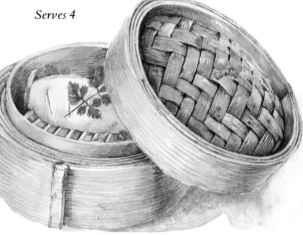

53

HOT APPLE CHUTNEY

*90g/3oz/a generous ½ cup chopped
onions
juice of 1 orange
90g/3oz/a generous ½ cup each of
diced carrots and celery
60g/2oz/4 tbsp dried apricots, chopped
45g/1½oz/3 tbsp raisins
30g/1oz crystallized ginger
3 tbsp cider vinegar*

*175g/16oz chopped dessert apples
(chopped weight)
a pinch of cayenne pepper or fresh
chopped chilli
ground mixed (black and white)
pepper
1 tbsp black treacle (molasses)
60g/2oz/½ cup roasted chopped
walnuts*

Stew the onion in the orange juice in a saucepan for 3 minutes with the lid on. Add carrots and celery and cook until they are *al dente*. Meanwhile soak the apricots with the raisins and crystallized ginger in the cider vinegar. Add the chopped apple and dried fruit in cider vinegar to the *al dente* vegetables. Then add the seasonings and cook gently for a further 3 minutes with the lid on the saucepan. Add the black treacle and stir well. Cook a little more if the mixture is too wet or the apple not cooked through (the apple should retain its shape). Just before serving stir the walnuts into the mixture. This chutney is particularly good served hot with boiled ham.

Makes 300ml/10fl oz/1¼ cups

GLAZED CARROTS AND APPLES

450g/1lb carrots
salt and freshly ground black pepper
450g/1lb dessert apples
30g/1oz/2 tbsp unsalted butter
1 tbsp granulated white sugar

Peel and cut carrots into batons (strips) 5cm/2inches long and 1cm/½inch thick. (If you use baby carrots they need only to be washed and trimmed.) Cook in boiling water with a pinch of salt until just tender (cooking time depends on the age of the carrots). Drain.

Peel, core and quarter the apples then cut the quarters into three thick slices. Put into the saucepan with the carrots, butter and sugar. Cook over a gentle heat to melt the butter and dissolve the sugar, turning the carrots and apples over as you do. Increase heat so that any moisture evaporates and the apples are softened slightly. When everything is covered with a shiny glaze, remove from the heat, season and serve.

Serves 4

ROAST PORK WITH STUFFED APPLES AND CIDER

1.5kg/3lb loin of pork, rind removed, chined
sprigs or leaves of sage
1 tbsp salt
1 tbsp fresh thyme
½ a bay leaf, crushed
300 ml/10fl oz/1¼ cups dry cider
freshly ground black pepper
about 4 tbsp finely chopped parsley
4 tbsp fine breadcrumbs
50g/2oz/¼ cup pine kernels
6 whole dried apricots, finely chopped
4 tbsp Calvados
½ tsp ground cinnamon
1 tbsp soft brown sugar
4 medium cooking apples
softened butter

Make small cuts in the pork and insert the sage sprigs or leaves. In a small bowl, mix together the salt and herbs and rub the mixture well into the joint. Cover and refrigerate overnight.

Preheat the oven to 190°C/375°F/Gas 5.

Tie up the meat for roasting; rub the herb mixture in again. Place the meat and the cider in a roasting tin (pan) and season with black pepper. Cover with greased paper or cooking foil and roast, fat side up for 1¼ hours,

basting occasionally. If the liquid evaporates, add a little more cider.

Meanwhile, prepare the stuffing for the apples. Mix together the pine kernels, apricots, Calvados, cinnamon and sugar in a small bowl. Set aside and leave to macerate for an hour or so.

Wipe each apple well, cut off their tops with a small knife and set aside. Remove the cores, taking care not to cut right through to the base. Lightly butter the cavity of each apple and fill with the apricot mixture; replace the tops of the apples.

Remove the meat from the oven and take off the paper. Mix the parsley and breadcrumbs together, and spread over the top of the meat, pressing it down gently with the flat side of a knife. Put the meat back in the roasting tin and arrange the apples round it. Spoon over any remaining Calvados. Reduce the heat to 160°C/325°F/Gas 3 and roast for a further 50–60 minutes, basting the meat with the liquid (adding a little more if it looks like drying out) and allowing the crumbs and parsley to form a golden crust.

Serves 4

APPLE GAMES

There were many games invented for Hallowe'en to keep people occupied inside while the witches and demons roamed around outside. One of these games was apple-bobbing, in which the apples were used as symbols of future fortune. Apples of varying sizes were floated in a tub of water, and the bobbers were blindfolded with their hands tied behind their backs and ducked under water to catch an apple with their teeth. The larger the apple caught the greater the fortune, and failure to catch an apple implied a life of poverty. At the same time, apples were roasted in front of the fire by suspending them on bobbin threads from the mantelpiece where they would twirl and sing while they cooked.

At Hallowe'en we played a combination of these two games. Apples suspended from thread tied to their stalks were attached at intervals to a horizontal pole, a child was placed in front of each apple – hands tied behind the back of course, but no blindfold – and whoever took the first bite was the winner, with a toffee apple as the reward.

On Hallowe'en night, in order to see her future husband's face, a young girl must look into the mirror while combing her hair and eating an apple. To find out his name, she must peel an apple and throw the unbroken peel over her left shoulder. The initial of her lover's name can be read from the twisted peel on the floor.

An apple-pie bed is a trick played by children (and sometimes by grown-ups). The top sheet is secretly folded in half and the bed re-made. The person getting into it suspects nothing until he tries to straighten his legs. Hairbrushes and pumice stones can be added for good measure and a thoroughly uncomfortable night.

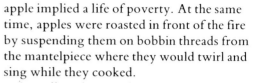

PUMPKIN WITH BULGUR WHEAT, APPLE AND NUT FILLING

A bright orange pumpkin is fun to serve as part of the Hallowe'en or Bonfire Night festivities. In Argentina pumpkins are filled with a rich beef stew, but this version uses combinations of fruit and nuts from the Caucasus.

1 pumpkin, 1.8-2.5kg/4-5lb
a little milk and sugar
sunflower oil
90g/3 oz/6 tbsp butter
2 tsp ground cumin
175g/6oz/1 cup bulgur wheat
450ml/15fl oz/scant 2 cups hot
vegetable or chicken stock
75g/2½oz prunes, roughly chopped
75g/2½ oz dried apricots, roughly chopped
90g/3oz/generous ½ cup whole
blanched almonds
2 dessert apples, peeled, cored and
diced
salt and freshly ground black pepper

Pre-heat the oven to 190°C/375°F/Gas 5.
Wash and cut a lid from the top of the
pumpkin, notching one side so it can slot
back on easily. Scoop out the seeds and fibre,
and make some shallow vertical cuts in the
flesh, making sure not to cut through the
skin. Paint the inside with milk and sugar
and the outside with a little sunflower
oil. Replace the lid, and place on a greased
baking sheet in the oven for 40–50 minutes
(allow more time for a larger pumpkin).
Melt half of the butter in a saucepan and fry
the cumin for 1 minute. Add the bulgur

wheat, coat with butter and cumin and sauté
until lightly browned, stirring constantly.
Add the stock, bring to the boil, and simmer,
covered, for 8–10 minutes.
Melt the remaining butter in a separate pan,
and sauté the dried fruit and nuts until
golden. Add the apple, and stir constantly
until the apple is golden but still firm. Mix
with the cooked bulgur wheat, and season.
Check that the pumpkin is cooked but not
collapsing. Fill the cavity, replace the lid and
put back in the oven for a further 15 minutes.
To serve, place on a large plate, and scoop out
the bulgur filling with the pumpkin flesh.

Serves 8

TOFFEE APPLES

Toffee apples are best made from small sweet apples.
It's fun for children to dip them in chopped
nuts, chocolate chips, toasted sesame or sunflower
seeds, or gem-sized pieces of crystallized fruit.

10 small dessert apples
250g/8oz/1 cup granulated sugar
2 tbsp golden (corn) syrup
1 tsp white wine vinegar
3 tbsp water
10 wooden sticks

Wash and dry the apples and remove the
stalks. Push a wooden stick into the centre of
the apple until it feels secure.

Put the sugar, syrup, vinegar and water into
a saucepan and heat gently until all the sugar
has dissolved. Increase the heat and boil
rapidly until the syrup forms little threads
when dropped from a spoon into cold water
(150°C/300°F). Remove from the heat.

Dip each apple into the toffee, turning to
coat it evenly. Either dip in any one of the
above suggested toppings or leave plain.
Stand the apples on an oiled baking tray to
cool and harden. Eat the same day.

Makes 10

APPLE AND STILTON STRUDEL

Although it sounds rich, the apples lighten the cheese enough to
serve this as a starter. It's great as a supper dish served with a crisp green salad or as
a main course for a vegetarian dinner party.

450g/1lb Russet or Cox apples,
peeled, cored and diced
juice of 1 lemon
1 tsp dried thyme
½ tsp freshly grated nutmeg
250g/8oz Stilton or Roquefort cheese
90g/3oz/¾ cup roasted chopped
walnuts
freshly ground black pepper
120g/4 oz/½ cup melted unsalted butter
90g/3oz/¾ cup dried breadcrumbs
4 large sheets of filo pastry

Preheat the oven to 190°C/375°F/Gas 5).
   Place the apple dice in a bowl and toss with
the lemon juice, thyme and nutmeg.
Crumble in the cheese and roasted walnuts.
Season to taste.
   Grease a 30cm/12 inch square baking sheet.
Unwrap the filo pastry and work quickly.
Place one sheet on the baking sheet, brush
with melted butter and sprinkle with one
third of the breadcrumbs. Keep the unused
pastry covered with a damp cloth. Layer the
filo sheets, brushing each with butter and
sprinkling with breadcrumbs. Do not
sprinkle crumbs on the top layer.

Serves 4–6

Drain the juices from the apple and cheese filling. Spoon the filling along one side of the filo, placing it about 5cm/2 inches from each of the long edges. Fold the long edges over the filling then fold the end flap over to enclose the filling. Gently roll up the strudel. Turn over so that the seam side is underneath. Brush with melted butter, then bake for about 30 minutes until the pastry is golden and the apples are tender. Remove from the oven, and brush with more melted butter. To serve, cool the strudel slightly and transfer to a serving dish.

Quince and Apple Soufflé

This recipe comes from *Jane Grigson's Fruit Book* and was invented by her daughter Sophie, who has kindly given permission to reproduce it.

250g/8oz quince
250g/8oz firm aromatic eating apples
2 cloves
15g/¹⁄₂ oz/1 tbsp, unsalted butter
caster (superfine) sugar
3 large eggs, separated
extra butter

Peel, core and cut the quince into small dice. Place in a heavy saucepan with a thin layer of water in the bottom. Peel, core and cut the apples into slightly larger pieces and put them on top of the quince, with the cloves. Cover and cook on a low to medium heat until the juices run and the fruit begins to soften. Raise the heat, and cook to a soft, dry mash, removing the lid if necessary.

Sieve the fruit, and add the butter and some sugar to taste. The purée should be on the sweet side. Mix in the egg yolks while the mixture is still warm.

Preheat the oven to 200°C/400°F/Gas 6. Put a baking sheet in the oven. Whisk the egg whites until they stand in peaks – they should not be too dry – then stir a spoonful into the fruit to slacken it, before carefully folding in the rest of the whites with a metal spoon or spatula, keeping as much air in the mixture as possible.

Butter a 1¾litre/3 pint/7½ cup soufflé dish generously. Put in a spoonful of sugar and turn the dish so the sugar coats it evenly; pour off any surplus or add more, if necessary. Turn the quince and apple mixture into the soufflé dish and slide it gently on to the baking sheet. Bake for 20 minutes.

Open the oven carefully. Pull out the baking sheet just far enough to sprinkle the top with sugar. Slide the tray back, close the oven carefully and bake for a further 5 minutes.

Serves 4

APPLE AND HONEY SORBET

250g/8oz/1 cup caster (superfine)
sugar
250ml/8fl oz/1 cup water
700g/1½lb dessert apples, weighed
after coring
juice of 1 lemon
120g/4oz/½ cup clear honey
1 egg white

Dissolve the sugar in the water over a low heat, then increase the heat and boil rapidly for 3–4 minutes without stirring. Turn off the heat and leave to cool.

Quarter the apples, leaving peel on a third of them (it flecks the sorbet prettily). Put in the food processor with the lemon juice, and process until puréed. Stir into the syrup with the honey until well combined, then pour into a shallow container. Freeze for 1–2 hours until mushy. Whisk the egg white stiffly. Take the sorbet out of the freezer, stir to soften, then fold in the egg white and re-freeze. Soften in the refrigerator for about 15 minutes before serving.

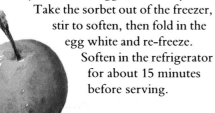

Serves 8

GINGER AND APPLE ICE CREAM

*700g/1½ lb apples, peeled, cored
and sliced
juice and finely grated rind of 1 lime
1 tbsp water
2 egg yolks
1 egg
300ml/10fl oz/1¼ cups milk or single
(light) cream
4tbsp ginger syrup
120g/4oz preserved ginger, chopped
300ml/10fl oz/1¼ cups double
(heavy) cream, whipped
2 tbsp icing (confectioner's) sugar*

Put the apples in a saucepan with the lime rind and juice and the water. Cook over a gentle heat, stirring occasionally, until reduced to a purée. Cool.

In a bowl beat together the egg yolks and whole egg with a wire whisk. Bring milk or cream to the boil, pour on to the eggs, whisking all the time, return to pan and cook very slowly, stirring constantly, over a low heat until custard thickens. Do not overheat, or the egg will curdle. Immediately it seems right, dip the base of the pan into cold water to prevent further cooking. Tip in the ginger syrup and stir in the apple purée. Freeze until firm.

Remove to a bowl and break up well. Fold in ginger pieces, whipped cream and sugar to taste. Return to freezer, stir again after 1 hour, then freeze until hard. Remove from freezer 20 minutes before serving.

Serves 8

FIG AND APPLE TARTS

I used these in the same recipe because the combination of purple and
gold was irresistible for painting.

FOR THE PASTRY
*220g/7oz/1¾ cups plain (all-
purpose) flour
60g/2oz/¼ cup icing
(confectioner's) sugar
pinch of salt
120g/4oz/½ cup softened butter
finely grated rind of 1 orange
2 egg yolks*

FOR THE FILLING
*900g/2lbs apples, peeled, cored
and sliced
juice of 1 orange
3 cloves
30-60g/1-2oz/2-4 tbsp caster
(superfine) sugar
2 large eggs
2 tbsp double (heavy) cream
6 fresh figs
6 tsps caster (superfine) sugar
icing (confectioner's) sugar and
Greek yogurt to serve*

Preheat the oven to
220°C/425°F/Gas 7.
To make the pastry,
mix flour, sugar and
salt together, and
rub in butter. Add
orange rind and
egg yolks and work
together to form a ball of dough.
Add a little water if it is too crumbly. Wrap in
greaseproof paper and chill for 30 minutes.

Roll out pastry and line six small round tins
10cm/4 inches in diameter, then chill for 10
minutes. Line with foil, weigh down with
beans and bake blind for 8 minutes. Take out
of oven remove foil and beans and brush with
a little beaten egg immediately to seal.
Reduce oven heat to 160°C/325°F/Gas 3.

To make the filling, put the apple slices,
orange juice and cloves into a saucepan. (Use
a mixture of dessert and cooking apples; the
purée will be flavoured with the sweetness of
the apple.) Cook over a low heat, stirring
frequently, until the apples have reduced to a
thick purée. Add sugar to taste, take off the
heat and remove the cloves.

Beat the eggs lightly with the cream and stir
into the apple purée. Fill the pastry cases with
this purée.

Cut the figs down from the top, making an X, leaving the segments attached at the bottom so that they open like flowers. Place these in the centre of the apple purée and press open. Sprinkle each fig with 1 tsp of sugar and bake tarts in the middle of the oven for 20 minutes until the purée is firm. Serve warm, sprinkled with icing sugar and with Greek yogurt on the side.

Serves 6

TARTE TATIN

A variation of the classic recipe invented by the sisters Tatin from the Solonge area of France. They caramelized their apple tart by cooking it in a covered metal tin (pan) on top of the stove.

FOR THE PASTRY
*150g/5oz/1¼ cups plain
(all-purpose) flour
120g/4oz/½ cup butter
1½ tbsp caster (superfine) sugar
pinch of salt*

FOR THE FILLING
*1kg/2lb Golden Delicious apples
60g/2oz/1¼ cup granulated sugar
1 tsp cinnamon
120g/4oz/½ cup butter
90g/3oz/⅓ cup sugar
crème fraîche to serve*

Rub the butter into the flour, sugar and salt, and gently combine into a ball. Wrap in greaseproof paper and chill for half an hour. Pre-heat oven to 180°C/350°F/Gas 4.

Mix together the cinnamon and sugar. Quarter, peel, core and slice the apples lengthwise and toss them in the sugar and cinnamon. Butter liberally a 22×6 cm/9×2½ inch deep baking dish. Sprinkle half the sugar in the base of the dish and arrange the apples over it, pouring over the melted butter as you go. Sprinkle the remaining sugar over the top layer of apples.

Roll out the pastry to 3mm/⅛ inch thick and cut to fit the dish, placing it over the apples with the edges falling on the inside of the dish. Cut 4 or 5 holes to allow steam to escape. Bake in the lower part of the oven for 45–60 minutes, protecting the pastry with foil if it begins to brown before apples are caramelized.

When cooked, cool slightly then turn out upside-down on to a serving dish and serve accompanied by a bowl of crème fraîche.

Serves 6–8

APPLE PIE

Every family has their own apple pie recipe. Here is ours.

FOR THE PASTRY
250g/8oz/2 cups plain (all-purpose) flour
1 level tsp baking powder (raising agent)
1 dsp icing (confectioner's) sugar
1 tsp salt
60g/2oz/¼ cup chilled butter, diced
60g/2oz/¼ cup vegetable shortening, diced
2-3 tbsp iced water
a little egg white, lightly beaten

FOR THE FILLING
700g/1½ lb cooking apples, peeled, cored and quartered
juice and finely grated rind of ½ lemon
90g/3oz/⅓ cup caster (superfine) sugar
3 cloves

Preheat the oven to 200°C/400°F/Gas 6.

For the pastry, sieve the flour, baking powder, icing sugar and salt into a bowl, then rub the butter and shortening into the flour until the mixture resembles breadcrumbs. Sprinkle in the water a little at a time, and stir in with a knife. Knead gently into a firm dough, wrap in greaseproof paper and chill for half an hour.

Roll out slightly less than half the pastry dough into a round which will line a 23cm/9 inch pie plate. Grease and line the plate with pastry and press gently all around. Paint edges with beaten egg white. Roll out the rest of the pastry for the lid.

Serves 6

Slice the apples very thinly on to the pastry base, sprinkling with lemon juice, rind and sugar as you go. Insert cloves at intervals. Brush the edges of the pastry with water and fit the top over the base. Trim all around, and crimp the edges together to seal them. Make a small opening in the top and decorate with pastry leaves made from the trimmings.

Bake in the middle of the preheated oven for 20 minutes then turn the oven down to 170°C/325°F/Gas 3. Bake for a further 20 minutes until golden brown. Sprinkle with extra sugar and serve hot with either cream or ice cream.

APPLE CAKE

3 tbsp hazelnuts
30g/1oz/2 tbsp butter
60g/2oz/½ cup plain (all-purpose) flour
2 tbsp light brown sugar
½ tsp ground cinnamon

FOR THE CAKE
120g/4oz/½ cup unsalted butter, softened
120g/4oz/generous ½ cup golden
caster (superfine) sugar
2 large eggs
250g/8oz/2 cups plain (all-purpose) flour
3 tsp baking powder
2 tbsp apple juice
4 drops vanilla extract
500g/1lb 2oz Cox's apples,
weighed when peeled, cored and
cut into 1cm/½ inch chunks

Put the hazelnuts on a baking sheet in the top of the oven until they are golden and the skins rub off easily. Remove skins and chop. Mix all the ingredients together with your fingertips until crumbs are formed. Sprinkle over the top of the cake.

Bake for 1–1¼ hours. Insert a fine knitting needle into the centre; if it comes out clean, the cake is cooked. Remove from oven. Leave in the tin for 10 minutes. Turn out, peel off the paper, and cool on a wire rack.

Preheat the oven to 170°C/325°F/Gas 3.

To make the cake, cream the butter and sugar together until they are light and fluffy, then beat in the eggs one at a time, sprinkled with a little of the flour. Sift the rest of the flour with the baking powder and fold in all but 30g/1oz/¼ cup of it, with the apple juice and vanilla extract.

Toss the apple in the remaining flour, and fold into the cake mixture. Put into a 20cm/8 inch loose-based oiled cake tin (pan), lined with an oiled greaseproof paper disc.

APPLE AND CHESTNUT BREAD

This bread is fun to bake in flowerpots and to serve straight from the oven to the table so that guests can unpot their own loaf. It is also delicious.

6 tbsp chestnut flour
400g/14oz/3½ cups strong white
plain (all-purpose) flour
2 tsp salt
1 tbsp golden caster (superfine) sugar
seeds from 5 cardamom pods
30g/1oz/2 tbsp butter
1 sachet easy-blend dried yeast
300ml/10fl oz/1¼ cups lukewarm water
6 tbsp chopped dessert apples
6 tbsp chopped cooked chestnuts

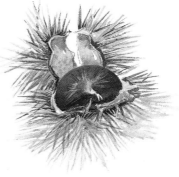

Pre-heat the oven to 190°C/375°F/Gas 5. Sieve the flours, salt and sugar into a large bowl. Grind the cardamom seeds in a mortar, and add them to the dry ingredients, then rub in the butter and add the easy-blend yeast. Make a well in the centre and pour in the water, mixing, so all the flour is incorporated. The dough should form a ball and come away clean from the sides of the bowl. (Add more water or flour if too dry or wet.) Knead for 5 minutes on a lightly floured surface, then put back into the bowl, cover with cling film and leave to rise in a warm place until doubled in size.

Dust apples and chestnuts with a little extra flour and knead these into the dough, knocking out all the air bubbles as you go.

Grease six sterilized flower pots 10cm/4 ins high. Divide dough into six pieces, shape into balls and press into the pots (the dough should be 2.5cm/1 inch from the top). Dust with flour, cover the pots and set aside in a warm place for the dough to rise above the rim of the pot.

Bake for 30–40 minutes in the lower part of the preheated oven until well risen and brown. (When baked, the loaf will sound hollow when turned out and knocked on the base.) Either turn out to cool on a wire rack or leave to cool for 10 minutes, then serve warm in the pot.

Makes 6 loaves

APPLE DRINKS

The main drinks made from apples are apple juice, cider and apple brandy. Apple juice is made from a mixture of varieties of crushed pressed dessert apples, and may or may not be carbonated. It is possible to buy pressed apple juice of a single named variety, and it is delightful to taste liquid Cox's Orange Pippin or Jonathan rather than just a generalized apple flavour. Cider came to Britain with the Celts and is a fermented liquor made from the juice of apples. It used to be made specifically from cider apples, which have a high tannin content and fibrous flesh with wonderful names like Redstreak, Foxwhelp and Strawberry Norman. The practice of spreading the pounded skin, flesh, pips and cores over the fields led to the growth of numerous seedlings, some of which yielded good cider apples which were then given names. Bess

Pool, for instance, is an apple good for cider and not bad for eating and was found growing wild in a wood by the girl who gave it her name. Unfortunately, most cider now is made from imported concentrates or dessert apples, and cider orchards are being torn out to make room for heavier yielding dessert bushes and old varieties are lost for ever. There is a huge range of ciders on the market: sweet and gassy, cloudy and flat and those which offer a more particular flavour and bite. It's worth exploring to find the few small cider-makers who remain true to their ancient craft and who produce characterful drinks from real cider apples.

Apple brandy is made by first fermenting then distilling apple juice. Calvados is the finest of all apple brandies, double distilled, then aged in oak casks for several years. It is the speciality of a region in Normandy from which it takes its name, where it is drunk after meals as well as a refresher between courses which are probably also cooked in it. Apple brandy from outside the controlled region may only be called *eau-de-vie de cidre*. Next to France, the United States is the world's most important producer of apple brandy. Sometimes called apple jack, it is produced in a variety of strengths, and is used in many long drinks and cocktails.

Cider vinegar is made from apple juice fermented into cider which is then exposed to the air and attacked by vinegar bacteria which sour it and convert it into acetic acid (i.e. vinegar). It has a strong taste of apple and can be used for preserving fruits and in chutneys. It is drunk by some weight lifters who appreciate its diuretic properties for revealing their muscles.

All of these apple products have culinary uses: they can be used in casseroles, as marinades, in vinaigrettes and in sauces. Juices and ciders improve if they are boiled down to half their original quantity before being added to a dish, as this intensifies their flavour.

85

YOGURT APPLE GINGER SHAKE

2 Granny Smith apples
375ml/12fl oz/1½ cups natural
yogurt
250ml/8fl oz/1 cup apple juice
2 tbsp ginger syrup from jar of
crystallized ginger

Chill all the ingredients. Peel, core and roughly
chop the apples. Place all the ingredients in a
blender and process until smooth. Taste
and add more ginger syrup if
necessary. Pour into a glass jug
containing ice cubes and serve.

Serves 4

CIDER CUP

1 litre/1¾ pints/1 quart dry cider
3 tbsp brandy
3 tbsp Cointreau
juice of 1 lemon
300ml/10fl oz/1¼ cups fresh orange
juice
orange and lemon slices

Chill the cider. Mix it with all the other ingredients in a large glass jug. Pour into glasses containing ice cubes and serve, with sparkling mineral water if preferred.

Serves 4

JACK ROSE COCKTAIL

60ml/2fl oz/¼ cup apple brandy
(Calvados or apple jack)
1 tbsp lime juice
a dash of Cointreau
sugar to taste

Shake with ice and strain into a cocktail glass.

Serves 1

SHAKER MULLED CIDER

3.4 litres/6 pints/3¾ quarts cider
1 tsp whole cloves
½ tsp freshly grated nutmeg
1 cinnamon stick
60g/2oz/¼ cup brown sugar

Put all the ingredients into a saucepan, bring to just below boiling point, but do *not* boil, and simmer for 5 minutes. Strain and serve in small mugs or glasses.

Serves 12

CRAB APPLE AND ROSEMARY JELLY

This jelly makes an attractive present. It is clear and amber-coloured,
with a sprig of fresh rosemary in each jar.

1.8kg/4lb crab apples
water to cover

granulated sugar to measure
sprigs of fresh rosemary

Wash the crab apples thoroughly. Cut into chunks, removing any bad bits. Put in a preserving pan and just cover with water. Simmer until the fruit is soft. Mash with a fork then strain through a jelly bag overnight.

For each 600 ml/1 pint/2½ cups of juice add 450g/1lb/2 cups of sugar to the preserving pan. Bring gently to the boil, stirring to dissolve the sugar, then boil rapidly until a temperature of 110°C/220°F (setting point) is reached (about 10 minutes). While the syrup is boiling swirl a large sprig of rosemary through it.

Remove from the heat and skim, put into jars, add a sprig of rosemary to each jar and seal, adding a decorative jam-pot cover.

Makes about 1.8kg/4lbs

CHEESE, APPLES AND WINE

In autumn and winter on special occasions a charming way to end a meal is to copy the Victorians and to make a display of as many varieties of the freshest, most colourful apples that you can find. They can be interspersed with seasonal berries – bright orange pyracantha looks particularly good though is itself inedible – decorative leaves and nuts, still in their pretty outer casings to open and to eat with the apples.

The classic combination is Stilton with Russet apples and aged tawny port. Here are some other suggestions:
– rich cream cheese with fruit bread, Fiesta apples and a New World Chardonnay;
– a young Lancashire or Caerphilly cheese with Worcester Pearmain or Discovery apples and Burgundy or Pinot Noir;
– the biggest chunk of Parmigiano Reggiano you can afford and the sweetest apples you can find to serve with Sauternes;
– goat's cheese with earthy Russets, nutty Pippins and Gewürztraminer;
– Emmental or Gruyère with Spartan apples and Californian Sauvignon blanc.

There are more combinations than there are apples (approximately 7,000 worldwide) so have fun.

INDEX OF RECIPE TITLES